# WALL ROMAN

## STAFFORDSHIRE

❖

Peter Ellis

*The Roman town at Wall, known to the Romans as Letocetum, lay on Watling Street, one of the main roads in Roman Britain. At first, the army established a succession of forts at the site. Later, a civilian settlement developed, as Wall became a key staging-post on Watling Street. Official travellers and postal couriers could change their horses and stay overnight in the guest house at Wall and make use of the neighbouring baths, the remains of which are still visible today. There is also a small museum displaying a selection of the items found at the site, including jewellery, pottery and a range of tools, which shed light on the lives of Wall's former inhabitants. The guidebook is divided in two sections, the first giving a detailed tour of the site and the second looking at the history of Wall.*

# ❖ CONTENTS ❖

*Published by English Heritage*
*23 Savile Row, London W1S 2ET*
*Copyright © English Heritage 1999*
*First published by English Heritage 1999*
*Reprinted 2004*

*Photographs by English Heritage Photographic Unit and copyright of English Heritage, unless otherwise stated. All objects are from Wall and are on display in the site museum, unless otherwise indicated.*

*Edited by Susannah Lawson*
*Designed by Derek Lee*
*Plans by Hardlines*
*Printed in the European Union by Snoeck-Ducaju & Zoon*
*C20, 6/04, FA4753, ISBN 1-85074-727-X*

# TOUR OF THE SITE

*Bird's-eye reconstruction drawing of the bath house and guest house, by Ivan Lapper*

## THE BATHS

*As you come out of the shop, walk across the grass towards the ruined remains and stop when you reach the sign marked 1. (The numbers in brackets in the text refer to the room numbers on the plan on p. 28.)*

You are looking at the excavated and consolidated remains of the Roman bath house. The surviving ruins include areas that were originally below floor level, so it is possible to see how the building worked and to get an idea of the simple yet effective technology involved in heating the baths.

Like all Roman baths, the bath house at Wall was a major architectural achievement. The building

*The walls of the bath house would once have been plastered and painted with patterns and scenes from mythology. These remaining, reconstructed fragments give some idea of what has been lost*

would have dominated its surroundings, giving off a cloud of steam in winter and even on the hottest day gently shimmering with heat. Inside, the rooms were all high and spacious, and the walls would have been plastered and then elaborately decorated with pictures showing gods and goddesses from Classical mythology, and also animal and flower motifs. Myths with sea subjects were often illustrated in baths, and fish designs are common. This remarkable building was maintained for over 150 years, despite undergoing several structural changes.

Large or small, Roman baths had the same simple layout, comprising a suite of rooms heated to varying degrees, with the hottest rooms nearest the furnace. Warm rooms were adjacent to the hot rooms, and at the entrances to the baths there were cold rooms with various types of cold baths. Within the baths, bathers went from room to room, usually in a clockwise sequence from the cold room through to the warm room and then to the hot room before returning to the cold room. The baths suites generally led off a large hall where bathers exercised to warm up before bathing. The hall was also used for educational activities, reading, learning, practising public speaking and so on, all regarded by the Romans as exercises for the care of one's health, and as important as physical exercise.

During the Roman period, the bath house was remodelled and extended on a number of occasions. The first bath house was built in about 100 AD (phase 1). It had a small exercise hall attached and ran up the slope rather than across it. Some of its rooms were incorporated in the later building while others lie beneath the grass on which you are standing. The baths were then extended to include the nearer suite of rooms in front of you (rooms 1–7 on the plan), with the exercise hall and some rooms retained from the earlier building (phase 2). This building phase is dated to the 130s AD at the time of the Emperor Hadrian. Later, a larger exercise hall was built and further rooms (8–12) were added some time in the 170s (phase 3). The furnace (7) was then converted into a warm room in the early third century (phase 4). All these developments were designed to make the baths more spacious and to add new facilities. Finally, in the later third century, the baths were reduced to a small nucleus of rooms (2–5 and 10–12), perhaps an indication of the desire to retain the baths despite a shortage of funds (phase 5). Later still, many of the doors were blocked and the building might have been used as a house. It was eventually abandoned, became ruinous and was finally buried beneath the fields.

*Turn left and walk along the grass beside the ruins. Stop at the end of the baths and look down the line of rooms.*

## The Furnace and Hot Room

The baths are made up of two suites of connecting rooms, set side by side (1–7 and 8–12). In the right-hand suite, the nearest room was the furnace room, called the *praefurnium* in Latin (1). A slow-burning fire, which would have been maintained night and day, was lit on the ground between the tile structures on the far side of the room. Hot air from the fire was drawn through the gap between the walls on either side of the main heat duct into the underfloor space beneath the two rooms beyond (2 and 3). This has now been infilled and grassed over, but formerly the floors of the rooms were supported by stacks of tiles, called *pilae* in Latin, around which the hot air circulated, heating the floor above. The fire also heated water in a large copper tank which was positioned directly over it on the tile supports. The first room beyond the furnace room was the hottest room, called the *caldarium* (2). At the near end there would have been a hot bath, or *alveus*, filled with water which was piped from the copper tank. The room beyond this was the warm room, or *tepidarium* (3). Although blocked when the baths were restored, the flues for drawing hot air beneath its floor can still be seen.

*Carry on walking up the hill and turn right at the far end of the bath house. Continue straight on until you reach sign 3.*

We will now follow the route taken by bathers through the baths. (For the purposes of the tour, it is assumed that the layout of the baths is as it was in phases 3 and 4, with earlier and later changes pointed out at the end of the description of each room.)

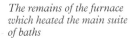

*The hot room and the warm room of the bath house*

*The remains of the furnace which heated the main suite of baths*

# ❖ THE ROLE OF THE BATHS ❖

To the Romans, going to the baths was an essential part of everyday life. The baths were a social institution, the place where people attended to their health, and where they could talk to their fellow citizens and discuss local issues and events. In the bath house everyone was equal – the social differences and distinctions of wealth evaporating in the steamy rooms. The only segregation was between men and women, who attended at different times of the day. The entrance fee was a small affordable sum and many people would have come daily, often spending the best part of the afternoon there. These fees might have supported the daily running costs, but the major costs of periodic repair and rebuilding were subsidised by the town or regional administration. Bath houses are found throughout the Empire from north Africa to Britain, and from Turkey to Portugal, with the largest concentration in Rome itself, where there were almost 900. These lavishly decorated buildings were an advertisement for everything the Empire stood for, including its power and the advantages of citizenship. Today, Turkish baths continue the bathing tradition.

The Baths of Caracalla in Rome, *a painting by Sir Lawrence Alma-Tadema (1836–1912)*

PRIVATE COLLECTION/BRIDGEMAN ART LIBRARY

## *The Exercise Hall*

You are now standing within the bath house exercise hall (13b). This was the town's main covered space and as well as being used for exercising it was also used for all kinds of meetings and entertainments. At certain times of the day, the room would have been used by trade guilds, for example, or by dining clubs – a popular Roman pastime.

*The site of the exercise hall, which was also used for meetings and entertainments*

School lessons might also have been held here. The discovery of bone dice, now on display in the site museum, suggests that people gambled here. For much of the period that the baths were in use, the room was also used as the changing room, or *apodyterium*, where bathers could leave their clothes with an attendant.

The hall was surrounded by a colonnade. The stone steps on the side of the building up the slope mark its entrance, and this lines up with the entrance to the baths directly across the hall. The floor would have been paved or tiled and excavation has shown that this was set on a thick layer of rubble carefully packed to form a level surface. At the far end of the building you can see where the wall of the larger hall has been butted on to the earlier smaller building, dating from phases 1 and 2. A drain can be seen running from this earlier room to the exterior.

*Turn left and go through the baths' entrance to sign 4.*

## The Cold Room, or Changing Room

From the exercise hall, bathers would have gone into this room, which was the cold room (8); it was also used as a changing room. The entrance passage had splayed sides narrowing towards the baths. On the left of the room was a cold bath (9), where the bather could start or finish with a dip in cold water. The grooved stones on either side of the entrance arch suggest that it was decorated. To the left of the doorway on the opposite side of the room was a semicircular alcove where there might have been a statue or a large water container. The walls of the room and the alcove were plastered with a thick cement mixture containing fragments of crushed tile, and surviving patches can still be seen. On the far side of the room, near the warm room (7), a drain was added late in the life of the baths to carry water from the cold rooms (5 and 6). The drain arch, now blocked, can be seen from the warm room (7).

*These bone dice, discovered near the exercise hall, suggest that gambling was a favourite pastime*

*The remains of the cold room, which was also used as a changing room*

*Reconstruction drawing of the changing room, by Ivan Lapper*

*Cutaway reconstruction drawing of the warm room with the hot room beyond, by Ivan Lapper*

The tiled break in the wall to the right of the entrance to the cold room marks the earlier entrance from the smaller hall. There was also an earlier wider door to its right into the lobby (10). This was then partly blocked, perhaps to reduce heat loss, and the alcove was cut into this blocking.

*Walk through into the lobby (10).*

## The Lobby

On the floor of the lobby is a stone lying where it fell from the upper part of the building. In the corner of the room, the large greensand stone would have acted as the base for the support of the roof vault. The blocking of part of the door between the cold room and the lobby (8 and 10) can best be seen looking back from inside the room. In an earlier phase, the room had been heated and the blocked hot air flues can be seen leading from the dry, hot room beyond (11). The door through to the next room that the bather would have used was later blocked off when the baths went out of use, so to re-join the bathers' path you will have to return to the cold room (8) and enter it from there.

*Return to the cold room (8) and walk though to sign 5.*

From here it is only possible to follow the bathers' course by climbing down into the underfloor heating areas. However, it is still possible to see the main features from sign 5 and then from the lobby (10).

## The Warm Room

From the lobby (10), the bather would have passed through the now blocked door into the warm room. It was originally a single room, but it was later divided into three rooms (4, 5 and 6). The cement plastering of the room is still visible in places. It was also possible to leave the main route followed by the bathers and go into a further warm room (7). Here, bathers might have been oiled by baths' attendants, presumably at additional expense for the use of the oils, which were kept in glass flasks.

In an earlier phase there was a furnace room in the further warm room (7) and the tiled sides of its flue are still visible low down beneath the wall between the two rooms. When the main warm room was partitioned, two cold rooms were provided (5 and 6) with a small cold water pool and a stone bench in one of the rooms (5), its base still visible where it is butted against the dividing wall. Water was drained from these rooms via the drain through the cold room (8).

*The remains of the tiled sides of a flue in the warm room, indicating that there was once an outlet to the exterior from this room*

## The Hot Room

From the warm room (4, 5 and 6), the bather would have entered the hot room (2 and 3). The floor level is indicated on the near wall on the right-hand side by a line of white cement. On the left-hand side there was an alcove where an urn containing hot water would have stood. At the far end of the room was a hot bath with water fed from the copper tank in the furnace room beyond. Here, bathers would have sluiced themselves down with hot water; water would also have been splashed across the heated floor, resulting in a moist, steamy atmosphere.

On the right-hand side of the hot room (3), a chimney carried the hot air from the underfloor space to the outside, in the building's second phase of development. This is marked by the sloping line of box tiles. In later stages, the alcove on the left-hand side was blocked with tiles and a wall was built across the room dividing it into two (2 and 3). At the far end on the right-hand side of room 2, the tile structures were added at a late stage when the original furnace room (1) had gone out of use and had been replaced by one next to it (12).

*Turn round and go back through the cold room (8) to the lobby (10).*

## The Dry, Hot Room

From the hot room, the bather would have returned to the warm room (4, 5

and 6), turned to his or her left and then gone through a door into the dry, hot room (11). Like the hot room (2 and 3), this room was heated, but it would have been a room of dry heat, called the *laconicum*, in contrast to the steamy heat of rooms 2 and 3. Here, bathers would have sat and sweated for a while, in the same way as in a modern sauna or Turkish bath. It can be seen from the two entrances from the lobby (10) that it was possible for bathers to bypass the main baths circuit and go only to the dry, heated room.

On the left-hand side of the dry, hot room and the furnace (11 and 12), it is possible to see what was originally the outside wall of the bath house when it comprised only rooms 1 to 7, during the second phase of its construction. The wall itself was set

*Diagram to show how the underfloor heating system in the baths worked*

*The blocked flues beneath the floor of the lobby*

*The remains of the cold plunge pool*

*View of the guest house from the north, with the remains of the dining room in the foreground*

*Reconstruction drawing of the guest house, by Ivan Lapper*

on a very wide base and was built progressively narrower the higher it went. It was also supported by masonry buttresses, an indication of the need to support the side walls with their heavy vaulted roofs. The blocking of the door into the dry, hot room (11), now supported by iron bands, took place when the building was no longer used as baths. The use of tile courses shows that the builders tried to retain the original design.

The dry, hot room (11) was heated from a furnace room beyond (12). In the left-hand far corner of the room, looking from the dry, hot room (11), steps led down from the exterior. On the right, a stone bench might have supported a water tank. At a later stage a second furnace to the left of the main one heated the hot room (2). A curved recess for the boiler was cut into the wall between the furnace (12) and the hot room (2). The flue leading through into the underfloor of the hot room (2) was subsequently blocked but the hole for the boiler pipe can still be seen.

## The Cold Room

From the dry, hot room (11), bathers returned to the lobby (10) and then through to the cold room (8). Here they would have been dowsed in buckets of cold water or they would have entered the cold plunge pool (9). They would then have had a final oiling and a scrape down by the baths' attendants using a strigil (a

curved metal instrument) before returning to the exercise hall (13b).

*Now leave the bath house and exercise hall and walk straight up the hill to sign 7.*

## THE GUEST HOUSE

The remains higher up the slope are those of a large building with rooms set round a courtyard. This was the guest house, called the *mansio*, where couriers on the imperial post system, the *cursus publicus*, could stay overnight. A courier had to have an official permit from the emperor which would have been issued by the province's governor. Normally they covered about 50 miles a day. In Britain it is likely that other public officials on business, and private citizens travelling along the great public roads, would also have been able to stop here. The buildings might also have been used for administrative purposes. Many of these guest houses had an attached bath house and thus the two buildings at

# ❖ AN EXTRAORDINARY DISCOVERY ❖

The most extraordinary find in excavating the guest house was a group of nine stones on which were carved human heads and figures. One of these figures is carrying a club – probably representing the Classical hero Hercules – and two others have shields. One of these stones is on display in the site museum and others can be seen in Birmingham City

*This stone with carved human heads was found at Wall. It seems to have come from an early second-century shrine, dedicated to a native god*

Museum. They seem to have come from an early second-century shrine, dedicated to a native god or gods but showing some Roman influences, which

was dismantled when the third guest house was built. The stones had been incorporated in a buried wall foundation to protect the new building, which was also guarded by a stone carving of a phallus, probably made at the time of building. There must therefore have been a religious shrine on this site which was then rebuilt elsewhere at Wall.

---

Wall are likely to have formed a single complex.

There were three successive guest houses on this site, and it is the third and last (built in the later second century, perhaps around the 170s) which is visible today. Unlike the baths, all the surviving interior walls are below the original floor levels, so no doorways or room entrances survive. Nothing remains to be seen of the two earlier buildings which were both of timber and comprised rooms laid out around an open, inner courtyard. The first building was constructed in about 80 AD (phase 1) and the second between 110 and 120 AD (phase 2). In the second phase of building, a well, about 2.5 metres

across and 7.5 metres deep, was sited in the middle of the courtyard. This lay beneath the later wall of room 14 which had to be bridged across it. Excavation of the well recovered quantities of red, blue, green, cream and gold wall plaster, suggesting that some of the rooms in the guest house were decorated with floral patterns in the second phase of construction.

*Walk to sign 8 and from here climb across the walls up to the gravelled areas within the building and then walk down to the far end beside the hedge.*

## The Entrance Hall

The building was approached from the side nearest the hedge. The long room there (21) would have been an

*The remains of three rooms in the guest house, perhaps the overseer's quarters*

open colonnade, its roof supported by columns. The entrance from the street into the entrance hall (20) via the colonnade (21) is marked by tiles, one with a finger-marked signature still visible. On the right-hand side of the entrance hall (20) was an office (2), and on the left was a wash room (3). This has a slot cut through its inside wall for a drain leading to a pit. The two hollows in the wall between the colonnade (21) and the main building might have been for good luck offerings when the building was under construction – other ritual deposits are known beneath the building (there is a similar hollow between rooms 13 and 14).

surround for a water container, perhaps with a fountain, or a statue base (19). On one side were ground-floor rooms to accommodate travellers. Rooms 5, 6 and 7 were the same size, with room 8 a little larger, to allow access from the internal corridor. These rooms would have had to contend with the problem of noise from the street and the baths. Room 4, on your left, was a staircase, leading to further accommodation on the first floor. On the right, rooms 1, 13, and 14 might have been the private accommodation of the overseer of the guest house. A step in the wall between rooms 13 and 14 may mark a lowered floor area. At the far end of the courtyard, rooms 10 and 11, as initially designed, would have been slightly superior guest rooms.

*Reconstruction drawing of the courtyard of the guest house, by Ivan Lapper*

## The Courtyard

The hall led through to an open courtyard (18) surrounded by a colonnade. Immediately in front of you, on entering the courtyard, the circular wall might have been the

*The remains of the courtyard of the guest house*

# ❖ DAILY LIFE: DINING AND FOOD ❖

The dining room, such as that in the guest house, was the most important domestic room for a Roman. In private houses and official buildings, meals were public affairs to which guests were invited and they were intended to demonstrate the influence of their host. Further down the social scale many people belonged to dining clubs and paid regular sums to enjoy occasional club meals. The home was not seen as a private area for the family but was open to visitors and acquaintances. In contrast, in the countryside, the home became more important for the family, and the types of pottery vessels reflect this change after the Roman Conquest from communal eating, a feature of Iron Age society, to a more private, family-based activity. In all classes, however basic the food, spices and spicy sauces were universally popular.

*A modern reconstruction of a typical Roman dining room, with decorated walls, low tables and a couch for reclining*

MUSEUM OF LONDON

## The Dining Room and Kitchen

The far end of the building from the entrance contained service rooms and an eating area. Room 12 was the largest and best-proportioned room and seems likely to have been the dining room with a kitchen nearby in room 16, and room 9 beyond as a service area. On three sides of room 12 were corridors of which only one part (17 on the plan) is visible. Underfloor heating was installed in the dining room (12) some time after its first building. The room was shortened and the external corridor

*The walls in the neighbouring village include stones re-used from the Roman town*

on the north side was blocked off. A furnace was constructed in the former corridor and hot air was drawn into channels beneath the room's floor. Access from the kitchen might then have been via room 10, which was divided by a wall.

## THE SITE MUSEUM

*To visit the museum, return to the shop and go down the path to the road, turn right and the museum is on the right, a few doors down.*

The objects on display in the museum are only a fraction of those found over the years. Most come from excavations carried out between 1912 and 1914. Pottery vessels include samian ware from Gaul and Germany, often stamped with the potter's name, *amphorae* – huge vessels for transporting wine – and mortars. Coins, brooches, beads, rings, studs, strap ends and pendants can also be seen, as well as toilet instruments used for cleaning ears and nails. Some examples of the building materials used are also on display, including window glass, iron fittings, painted wall-plaster, column bases and capitals. The stamped tiles from the baths marked PS (perhaps the initials of the maker) are datable to the reign of the Emperor Hadrian.

*A bronze statuette of a wrestler, half-melted from a fire*

*A tile found in the bath house, stamped with the initials 'PS', perhaps the initials of the maker*

## THE VILLAGE OF WALL

*To visit the village, turn left at the site entrance and walk up the road until you come to the Trooper Inn. Turn left up Green Lane.*

This road which runs from the Trooper Inn up to the church, runs along the west side of a fourth-century walled enclosure and is lined with stones which perhaps came from it, or possibly from the Friary at Lichfield. More stones can be seen in the bottom course of Pear Tree Cottage (on the Market Lane side) and, past the church, in the stones by the side of the driveway at the entrance to Wall House Barn.

*Walk back to the Trooper Inn and then turn left.*

Further stones can be seen reused in field boundaries and in Manor Farm at the crossroads (built 1636–9). There are no further extant Roman ruins although the banks of the fourth-century enclosure can be seen in places to the south of Watling Street. Building works on either side of the road often produce buried remains, as does ploughing in the nearby fields.

# HISTORY OF WALL

## WALL IN THE IRON AGE

Wall lies on the frontier between two Iron Age tribes – the Cornovii to the west and the Corieltauvi to the east. An ancient, pre-Roman route runs between the two tribes near Wall, and there is some evidence that there was a track off the main route, leading to Wall itself. Although no evidence for an Iron Age settlement has been found at Wall, the surrounding countryside must have been relatively well-populated in the Iron Age, as there are a number of hillforts in the area, and there is evidence of agriculture and fields from plough furrows found beneath the guest house. Moreover, the stones reused in the guest house indicate the location of an early Romano-British religious shrine, which is likely to have had an Iron Age predecessor.

The Roman name for Wall, Letocetum, came from the Iron Age name for a grey wood. This need not necessarily imply that the whole area was heavily wooded, and, as elsewhere in southern England, the late Iron Age landscape would have been one of fields, hedgerows, and tracks between settlements and farmsteads. The 'grey wood' might in fact have been referring to a sacred grove at Wall. Iron Age religious sites were often located on the frontiers between tribes and they attracted periodic markets and fairs. This might have been the origin of Wall.

## THE ARRIVAL OF THE ROMAN ARMY

A few years after the Romans had landed in Kent in 43 AD, a detachment of troops arrived in the Wall area and set up an overnight camp. The troops would have been on the western border of the Corieltauvi tribe and they might have been advancing into territories that had already sided with Rome. At least two of these so-called marching camps are known near Wall from aerial photographs. They were

*These quernstones, found at Wall, would once have been used for grinding corn*

*Aerial view of Wall, with the baths and the guest house on the left*

strict lines, according to a standard pattern.

By the late 40s, troops advancing north and west from London established more permanent forts along the route, as they brought supplies for their campaigns in Wales. It had, by the early 50s, become the major road between London, Wroxeter and Chester, and was later known as Watling Street.

At Wall, a fortress to accommodate part of a legion was laid out across Watling Street in the early 50s. Its defences have not been located, but parts of a timber-framed barrack

rectangular areas, defended by an earthwork bank and ditch; the soldiers would pitch their leather tents here, in

# ❖ WATLING STREET AND ROMAN ROADS ❖

*Roads were crucial to the development of the Roman Empire. This inscribed stone was once part of a road marker, showing the distance between towns*

The Roman Empire depended on its roads. Without a good communication system, army units could not be rapidly deployed, decisions could not be swiftly carried out and taxes could not be collected efficiently. Rapid journeys were made in small mule-drawn carts and journeys of 700 miles in 6 days and 200 in 24 hours are known elsewhere in the Empire. The roads were great engineering achievements, generally set on a raised bank. At Wall, the straight line of Watling Street

was maintained even across boggy ground.

The original choice of routes made by the Roman army in the first century AD has dominated the English road system since, with Watling Street transformed today into the A5. Until the railways came this was the key route from London to north Wales and Ireland. The Roman road names are unknown; 'Watling' and 'Ryknild' are Saxon in origin, their derivations and meaning also unknown.

block, a granary building and a succession of possible store buildings
have been found together with
hearths and latrines. The fort would
have accommodated part of the Legio
XIV Gemina, a legion that had come
to Britain from Mainz in Germany
and campaigned in the West
Midlands before moving to a
legionary fortress at Wroxeter in the
60s. The choice of the Wall area for
this and other forts suggests that local
agriculture was able to supply most of
the soldiers' needs.

East of Wall, a second major
Roman route, Ryknild Street, had
been established by the early 60s.
This carried traffic from the south-
west and connected Wall with
Roman forts at Metchley in Birmingham to the south, and at Derby to
the north.

The fort at Wall was thoroughly
cleared when the camp was
abandoned by the end of the 50s. By
then, Roman control had extended
into north Wales but the smooth
progress of its imposition was
violently interrupted when the
British in the South-east rose in
revolt under Boudicca the widow of
Prasutagus, a king of the Iceni in
what is now East Anglia. A new fort
at Wall was established in response
to the rebellion. It was located on a
new site away from the road, which
must therefore have become increas-
ingly devoted to civilian use. The
new camp lay to the north-west on

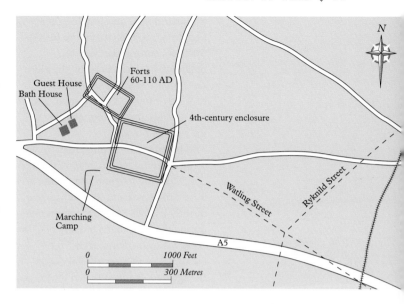

the hilltop, where the village and
church are today. Within the fort,
barrack blocks were once again
found. These were timber-framed
with wattle and daub walls and they
were constructed according to a
standard plan, with sleeping quarters
linked by an outside veranda with
storage areas for weapons.

Once the revolt had been sup-
pressed, this second fort was cleared,
its defences levelled and its buildings
burnt. Subsequently, two further
forts with multiple defensive ditches
are known, both on the same site as
the Boudiccan fort, and both set in
successively smaller areas within it.
In the first of these, the barrack
buildings were replaced by a
centurion's quarters. This fort too

*A map of Wall, showing its
position west of the junction
of Watling Street and
Ryknild Street*

was abandoned and levelled. In a final fort, probably from the turn of the first century, the previous buildings were replaced by the close-set timber joists of a solid floor, probably intended for storage. This fort was finally abandoned early in the second century.

These later forts might have been involved in military activity in the 70s, when the Brigantes to the north were conquered and then subsequently used as back-up stations during the campaigns of Agricola, the governor of Britannia from 78 to 84 AD. Later they would have acted as storage depots for troops in the North. At the same time a civilian settlement came into existence beside Watling Street.

*This mixing bowl, found at Wall, was once used for preparing food*

## The Civilian Settlement

The name of the settlement at Wall was 'Letocetum'. We know this from two Roman documents: the *Antonine Itinerary*, which was a third-century list of roads and staging-posts in the Empire, and the *Ravenna Cosmography*, a description of the Empire from the seventh century. The name was not new, but a Romanization of an earlier Iron Age name meaning 'grey wood' ('leto', or 'llwyd' in Welsh, meaning grey, and 'cetum', or 'coed' in Welsh, meaning 'wood'). The name might have referred to an area centred on Wall rather than to Wall itself.

*The discovery of these glass beads and (top right) iron nails and tools suggests industrial activity at Wall*

Soon after 70 AD, Watling Street was constructed with a gravelled surface. A section across it west of the junction with Ryknild Street showed that it had been pushed in a straight line across the edge of a former area of wetland. This line was marked by a layer of peat bog onto which the Roman engineers laid a 27-foot wide layer of sand and gravel. The road surface survives better in the area of the first Roman fort where it was laid across the trenches of the fort buildings.

On all the military sites at Wall, army occupation was rapidly followed by civilian buildings and industrial activity. From the first half of the second century, a number of timber buildings have been discovered together with hearths, and there is evidence of metal-working. In particular, evidence of glass-working and glass-blowing was found to the west of the road junction at Castle Croft:

# ❖ ROMAN TRADES AND CRAFTS ❖

As well as being used by imperial couriers, private travellers and local people coming to the town markets, Watling Street was also used for the long-distance transportation of materials. Mule trains or ox-drawn carts would have carried pottery, oysters (carried live), wine, oil, spices, relishes, quernstones, stone mortars and stone for building. At Wall the stone came from Lichfield and Hopwas, while lime for cement came from quarries near Walsall. Farms would have brought produce into Wall, and animals would have been

*Glass was made at Wall. This blue glass jar, on display in the site museum, would once have been used for storing ointment*

driven in to slaughter houses in the town. Metal-, bone- and leather-working was common

at Wall. A group of wheel-wright's and farrier's tools found at the guest house indicates a specialisation in transport services. Food would also have been sold in shops alongside the road. There is also evidence of glass-, tile- and pottery-making at Wall. These activities would have been undertaken away from occupied areas to reduce the risk of fire.

waste material called 'moiles' were found, as were tails of molten glass, which must have been caught in the workmen's pliers; there were also vessel fragments gathered for reuse or rejected by the glass-maker.

Both Celtic and Latin would have been spoken at Wall, with Celtic the language of everyday and Latin the written and administrative language. Most inhabitants of Wall, sited as it was on a major road, and so in contact with the Province as a whole, would have been bilingual.

## THE BATHS AND GUEST HOUSE

The most important buildings at Wall in the early civilian years were the baths and the guest house, which are still visible today. They owe their existence entirely to Watling Street. The Empire's success was vitally linked to its road system. To maintain communications, official travellers and postal couriers could change horses or mules at set points and stay overnight at guest houses such as the one at Wall.

*General view of Wall, with the guest house in the middle ground*

These were to be maintained by the tribes on whose land they lay. In the *Antonine Itinerary*, Wall is listed along with Pennocrucium (near Penkridge) and Mancetter to the west and east, where there were changing stations but no official accommodation.

The guest house had bedrooms, offices, an overseer's suite, a dining room and kitchen on the ground floor, and, presumably, further accommodation on the first floor. This was a big establishment devoted to the comfort of imperial officials and the better off, whose progress through what must have seemed semi-barbaric countryside could thus have been broken by a decent bed and by dinner and conversation with their fellow travellers and officials from the local administration. They could also visit the attached bath house, and continue on the road reinvigorated and with fresh transport.

Although the baths were clearly closely linked to the guest house, they were not used exclusively by its occupants. The baths would have closed at night but the fires would have been kept alight twenty-four hours a day in order to maintain the through draught of hot air. The baths must also have been used by the townspeople, perhaps with certain times set aside for use by the guest house.

The baths and guest house are not aligned with Watling Street. The entrance to the later guest house, and presumably to the earlier ones, was on the east side, and this would have opened onto a road leaving Watling Street at an angle and running up to the forts on the hilltop. This route might have been Iron Age in origin. The position of the guest house and the baths on the hillside would have presented a striking picture to a traveller coming from the west.

The first guest house at Wall was made of timber and is dated to the 70s or 80s AD. The bath house, constructed of stone from the outset, was built in about 100 AD as an addition to the guest house, its water supply coming from a spring line above the guest house. However, soon after the bath house was constructed, the first guest house was destroyed by fire and it was replaced by a second building. Like its predecessor this too was made of timber.

Near the new guest house there was a Romano-British shrine or temple; the stone from this was reused in the third guest house. The shrine

*A road ran between the bath house and the guest house*

# ❖ RELIGION AND BURIAL ❖

Religion and religious practices were an integral part of everyday Roman life. Shrines were present in every house and at street corners, with more important cult centres, like the one known near the guest house, visited on special days. In Britain, the gods and goddesses worshipped were Iron Age in origin but they were given Romanized names and attributes.

Burial was not permitted within domestic areas, but the dead were regarded as remaining part of the community and could not be left friendless and isolated. They were therefore buried or cremated just outside towns. The only exceptions are infant burials, often found in the foundations of domestic buildings. At Wall there is one known burial area about 500 metres west of the guest house and baths. Cremated bones were placed in pottery, metal or glass vessels.

*This funerary urn, on display in the site museum, was found just outside the boundary of the town*

might have been built entirely of stone or wood with a stone facade or arcade. There is a possibility that the large well in the second guest house also had a religious significance. The surviving stones from the building were decorated in the style of native rather than Roman craftspeople, although the shrine itself would have been a Romanized structure. The Romanization of native religious practices was very common in the Empire and so an original Iron Age religious focus is likely.

The bath house was replaced in the 130s and the new building can be dated by the use of stamped tiles to the reign of Hadrian (117–138 AD).

The layout of the second bath house was different from the first and more rooms were added.

At some time in the later second century, perhaps in the 170s, the shrine was moved, the guest house was completely rebuilt, and the bath house was remodelled to include a much larger hall and three further rooms including a dry, hot room.

The baths were again enlarged at the beginning of the third century with the conversion of a furnace to a warm room (7). The stone guest house was destroyed some time in the third century after a lifespan of perhaps sixty or seventy years. It was not replaced and there is no evidence

*View of the guest house from the south with the remains of the colonnade in the foreground*

for any further use of the site in the Roman period. Imperial travellers were now presumably lodged in private houses. The failure to replace the guest house is an indication of the difficulties the provincial government had in raising money from the local tribes to maintain the imperial infrastructure. However, despite the disappearance of the guest house, the baths continued to be used, albeit in a modified version, with three heated rooms and a cold room. The earlier furnace room had to be abandoned and new heating flues were punched through existing walls. The exercise hall was no longer in use. After the baths were abandoned, the building was still maintained, perhaps as a dwelling.

## WALL IN THE LATER ROMAN PERIOD

While the public buildings at Wall encouraged the successful development of the town, Wall's position near a major crossroads must also have contributed to its commercial success. Local farmers could have brought their produce to market here, imperial administrators could have assessed and gathered taxes, and here travellers could have stayed overnight. Archaeology has also shown that Wall was an industrial centre producing glass, pottery and metalwork. These goods would have been sold at local markets which could easily have been reached along Watling Street and Ryknild Street.

*Reconstruction drawing of the street between the guest house and the bath house (on the right), with its market stalls, by Ivan Lapper*

# ❖ LEGENDS FROM WALL ❖

A subterranean passage is reported to lead from the Butts to Castle Croft and an unsuccessful search for it was made in 1872. Passageways are often reported at Roman sites, especially near bath houses, and they may result from the finding of stone culverts or wells such as the one discovered behind the Trooper Inn in 1914. This was cleared to a depth of 15 metres in 1925–6. The subterranean passage searched for in 1872 could possibly have been the well beneath the guest house. Another often repeated story from Wall concerns the finding by road-menders near the church of a life-size earthen-ware statue of 'a woman's figure in a strange dress with a man's cap like a soldier's helmet'. The object was then broken into pieces to mend a drain. The story might have led on to the widespread reports that a temple of Minerva lies on the slopes below the church. Perhaps there is some connection between the reports and the location of the sacred site after it was moved from near the guest house.

A number of domestic buildings have been discovered at Wall over the years. The most interesting one was a sandstone building dating to the third century and subsequently destroyed by fire. An iron window grille and a pane of glass had fallen into the building in its collapse. The window grille suggests that the building was a strong-room, perhaps for official items, or part of a wealthy town house. It was replaced by timber-framed buildings. Other Romano-British buildings, mostly timber-framed but some at least partly of stone, have been found on the south side of Watling Street west of the guest house, and also to the east, towards the junction of Watling Street and Ryknild Street.

Pottery and building debris has been found along Watling Street, stretching for over 1.5 kilometres and up to 200 metres back from the road, suggesting that this was the extent of the town. Industrial activity was widespread, with iron and copper-working, pottery and tile production and glass-making. Excavation has located a number of gravel streets. The limits of the town may be indicated by cremation burials from the early Roman period lying 500 metres beyond the westernmost known buildings. Roman cemeteries generally occur at the town or city limits, indicating that the town

*Pottery and building debris has been found along Watling Street. This red samian ware bowl, terra-cotta jug and column capital are typical of the range of objects unearthed at Wall*

extended for as much as two kilometres along Watling Street.

There might have been a wealthy suburb round the guest house in Roman times, dedicated to higher-class residency and administration, and a commercial area to the east towards the road junction. The fort areas on the hilltop, where the village lies today, seem to have been little occupied after the second century, although the evidence may well be masked by the present buildings.

In the fourth century, many of the farmsteads in the region were abandoned, and it is possible that Wall and the area around it was in decline before the end of Roman Britain in the early fifth century. The financial demands made on Wall in the earlier Roman period, to supply accommodation and transport to officials on the road, might have become too much to support, and, in the later Roman period, the town might have lost its semi-official function and could have ceased to supply a service to travellers.

Wall is the site of one of the earliest pieces of evidence of Christianity in the region: a bronze bowl (now lost) was discovered with a 'Chi-rho' symbol embossed on the base (these are the Greek letters which stand for the first two letters of Christ's name). It seems to have been found in a stone-lined grave, thus indicating an early Christian community at Wall.

*These Roman coins were found at Wall. They date from the later Roman period*

## THE FOURTH-CENTURY DEFENCES

There was one important addition to late-Roman Wall. At some point in the early fourth century, a rectangular enclosure was built across the road. This was marked by a massive sandstone wall fronting an earthen rampart with three ditches in front of it. The entrances on Watling Street must have been protected by gates. The enclosure was laid out across earlier houses and a well. Very little occupation evidence has been found to accompany the defences although a few late fourth-century coins and a small section of a street with building debris on it have been recorded. Since there is no evidence of fourth-century activity outside the enclosure it would seem that the existing straggle of shops and houses alongside Watling Street was abandoned and the community resettled within the enclosure. Four similar enclosures are

known on Watling Street between Towcester and Wroxeter. They have been thought of as military defences with parallels on the Continent but this now seems unlikely. The Watling Street enclosures might have been established for commercial reasons in order to maximise rents and tolls.

Despite the lack of evidence of occupation from its interior, the fourth-century enclosure might have remained in use into the post-Roman period. A seventh-century poem records an attack on a place called 'Caer Luitcoed' by a cattle-raiding party from Wales, and this is thought to be referring to the defended enclosure at Wall which might, by then, have been the focal point of a monastic community. The raid was led by Moriael of Ercall and the poem celebrates the fact that, despite 'slumbering bishops' and 'book bound monks', Moriael got away with 500 oxen and 80 horses. The Iron Age, Roman and Welsh name of 'Letocetum' or 'Lwytgoed' appears in this period as 'Luitcoed' or 'Luitcoyt'. This was then transferred to 'Lichfield', by an Anglo-Saxon conversion into 'Lyccid' and then 'Lichfield'. This name migration tends to suggest that Letocetum was the name of an area rather than a place. This might have originated as a late-Roman estate, perhaps the territory of a tribal sub-group of the Cornovii, which appears centuries later in the *Domesday Book* as the Bishop of Chester's manor of Lichfield. By then, Lichfield was the regional centre and no settlement was recorded at Wall.

## WALL IN MEDIEVAL AND LATER TIMES

The manor of Wall was formed between 1135 and 1166 out of the manor of Lichfield and there are subsequent references to the lords of Wall during the medieval period. The present Wall House may mark the site of their manor house. The earliest surviving buildings in Wall date to the seventeenth century when twelve house owners were recorded in the hearth tax assessment of 1666. The first mention of Roman remains is in 1686, when coins and pavements were recorded. The antiquarian William Stukeley saw ruined walls in the process of being pulled down to build new houses in the eighteenth century. The Roman walls might have given modern Wall its name, or the name might have come from the Saxon word for a spring. Today, Wall is spared the through traffic on the A5, but the bypass is a reminder of a continuing route now almost 2000 years old which, in the first centuries of its existence, gave rise to a successful Roman settlement.

# BIBLIOGRAPHY

E. Black, *Cursus Publicus: the Infrastructure of Government in Roman Britain*, Oxford, 1995

B. Burnham and J. Wacher, *The Small Towns of Roman Britain*, Berkeley, CA, 1990

S. Frere, *Britannia: a History of the Roman Empire*, London, 1987

G. Webster, 'The Bath-house at Wall', *Transactions of the Birmingham Archaeological Society*, 74, 1958, pp.12–25

F. Yegul, *Baths and Bathing in Classical Antiquity*, Cambridge, MA, 1992

The main excavations at Wall, by A. Round, J. Gould, and F. and N. Ball, are to be found in volumes of the Transactions of the South Staffordshire Archaeological Society, especially volumes 5, 8, 15, 23, 32 and 38.

The following are gratefully thanked for their help: Frank and Nancy Ball, Steven Campbell-Kelly, Jim Gould, Martin Henig, Alex Jones, Sara Lunt, Alan Moore, Nigel Philpott, and Diana Wilkes.

| Roman Empire/Britannia | |
|---|---|
| 55–4 BC | Two expeditions of Julius Caesar |
| 43 AD | Claudius's invasion of Britain |
| 54–68 AD | Emperor Nero |
| 60–1 AD | Revolt of Boudicca |
| 70 AD | Construction of Watling Street and possibly Ryknild Street |
| 79 AD | Destruction of Pompeii |
| 78–84 AD | Agricola's campaigns in the North |
| 117–138 AD | Emperor Hadrian |
| 120/1 AD | Construction of Hadrian's Wall |
| 143 AD | Construction of the Antonine Wall |
| 216/17 AD | Baths of Caracalla in Rome |
| 306–37 AD | Emperor Constantine I |
| 379–95 AD | Emperor Theodosius I |
| 395 AD | Division of Empire into East and West |
| C5th | Departure of army from Britannia |
| C5–7th | Independent kingdoms in the west |
| C7th | Growth of Lichfield |

| Wall | |
|---|---|
| 44–50 AD | Marching camps |
| 50s AD | Legio XIV fort |
| 60–1 AD | First hilltop fort |
| 70s AD | Second hilltop fort |
| 80 AD | First guest house |
| 80s AD | Third hilltop fort |
| 100 AD | First bath house (phase 1) |
| 110s AD | Departure of military; second guest house |
| 130s AD | Second bath house (phase 2) |
| 170s AD | Third guest house; third bath house (phase 3) |
| c 210 AD | Fourth bath house (phase 4) |
| 250 AD | Disuse of guest house |
| c 275 AD | Fifth bath house (phase 5); stone building with grille |
| c 300 AD | Domestic reuse of baths building |
| c 325 AD | Walled enclosure |
| c 655 AD | Attack on Caer Luitcoed |

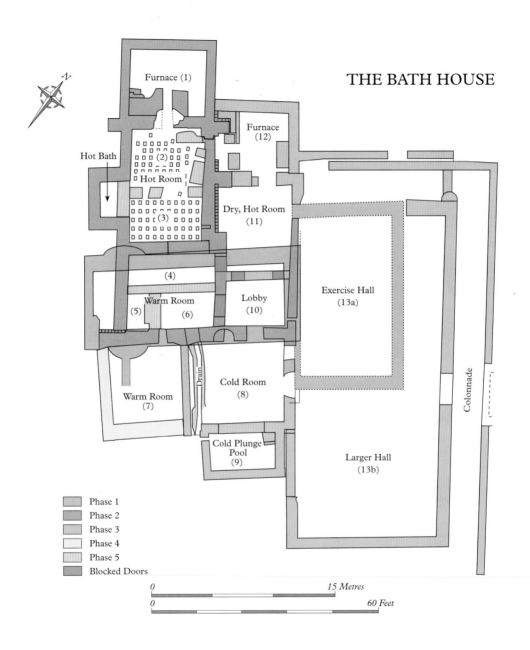

THE BATH HOUSE

Furnace (1)

Furnace (12)

Hot Bath

(2)

Hot Room

Dry, Hot Room (11)

(3)

(4)

Warm Room (6)

(5)

Lobby (10)

Exercise Hall (13a)

Drain

Cold Room (8)

Warm Room (7)

Cold Plunge Pool (9)

Larger Hall (13b)

Colonnade

Phase 1
Phase 2
Phase 3
Phase 4
Phase 5
Blocked Doors

0                    15 Metres

0                              60 Feet